Friends Should Know
When They're Not Wanted

Pearls Before Swine Collections

Because Sometimes You Just Gotta Draw a Cover With Your Left Hand

Larry in Wonderland

When Pigs Fly

50,000,000 Pearls Fans Can't Be Wrong

The Saturday Evening Pearls

Macho Macho Animals

The Sopratos

Da Brudderhood of Zeeba Zeeba Eata

The Ratvolution Will Not Be Televised

Nighthogs

This Little Piggy Stayed Home

BLTs Taste So Darn Good

Treasuries

Pearls Freaks the #%# Out*

Pearls Blows Up

Pearls Sells Out

The Crass Menagerie

Lions and Tigers and Crocs, Oh My!

Sgt. Piggy's Lonely Hearts Club Comic

Gift Book

Da Crockydile Book o' Frendsheep

Friends Should Know When They're Not Wanted

A SOCIOPATH'S GUIDE TO FRIENDSHIP

by Stephan Pastis

**Andrews McMeel
Publishing, LLC**

Kansas City • Sydney • London

Andrews McMeel Publishing, LLC
an Andrews McMeel Universal company
1130 Walnut Street, Kansas City, Missouri 64106

www.andrewsmcmeel.com

12 13 14 15 16 WKT 10 9 8 7 6 5 4 3 2 1

ISBN: 978-1-4494-0117-7

Library of Congress Control Number: 2011926174

Attention: Schools and Businesses

Andrews McMeel books are available at quantity discounts with bulk purchase for educational, business, or sales promotional use. For information, please e-mail the Andrews McMeel Publishing Special Sales Department: specialsales@amuniversal.com

Friends Should Know When They're Not Wanted

A friend is someone you can
tell anything.

Though if it's "I slept with your mother
and sh*t in the Thanksgiving turkey,"
there'll probably be ramifications.

A good friend warns you when your stalker is violating his restraining order.

Friends don't text you with
"Have u banged her yet?"
while you're still out on the date.

A friend is someone who puts the needs of others above their own.

Find one of those people and take advantage of them.

Friends stand right there beside you.

Which is too bad when they're dressed like this.

Friendships are like rainbows.

They go away.

Friends are there to comfort you.
Until you leave the room.

Then they call you "whiny."

There is no greater joy in life than the simple act of laughing with a friend.

Except laughing AT him. That rocks.

Be a friend to the elderly.
But don't get too friendly.
They'll die soon.

"I've got your back"
is a reassuring phrase from a friend.

It's less reassuring when you're the weakest man on a lifeboat and your friends are divvying up the meat.

A friend's advice is like the gentle coo of a dove.

Annoying and repetitive.

Good friends remember to only THINK you're a slut and not say it out loud.

When friends begin a sentence
with the phrase "To be honest,"
I always want to reply, "Were you
bullsh*tting the rest of the time?"

Friends don't touch
every single bun before deciding on
which one they want.

A friend is someone
who can call you at 4 a.m.

Which is why you should
turn off your phone at night.

With a friend, you're never alone.
Though you'll often wish you were.

Friends spend your special day with you.

Which is why it's so easy for them to ruin it.

A friend reveals himself
in times of need. His need.

Which is why you should turn off the
lights and pretend you're not home.

Friends remember to
shut the f**k up now and then.

Friends are like seagulls.

Sometimes they crap on you.

*Friends don't dwell on
each other's faults.
For that, we have spouses.*

True friends last a lifetime.

So does chronic back pain.

Friends celebrate
each other's differences.

Until they celebrate too much
and slip and say something racist.

No success can be truly enjoyed
unless it is shared with others.

It's called gloating.

They say that one loyal friend
is better than ten thousand relatives.

But what's NOT better than
ten thousand relatives?

A friend is someone who
accepts you as you are.

So be as difficult as possible.

Friends know when to say when.

Friends share.

So when they're not looking,
rifle through their wallet.

Friends should know
when they're not wanted.

You can't put a price on a friend.

Which is too bad.
I'd like to sell mine.

Being a friend means answering the phone in someone's time of need.

Unless they keep calling. Then just fake a Mexican accent and say, "Wrongo numero."

There is nothing more enjoyable
than a friend's success.

Except his failure.
That's pretty fun.

They say that every good friend
was once a stranger.

Which is also true of most serial killers.

They say that friends make you rich.

So try using one as a down payment on a house and see how far that gets you.

Friends don't photobomb
the only picture taken
at your fifth birthday party.

Friends listen.

Which is why you need to say,
"Hey weirdo, mind your own
f**king business."

Friends don't let friends
wear their collar up.

They say a man's friendships
are the best measure
of his wealth.

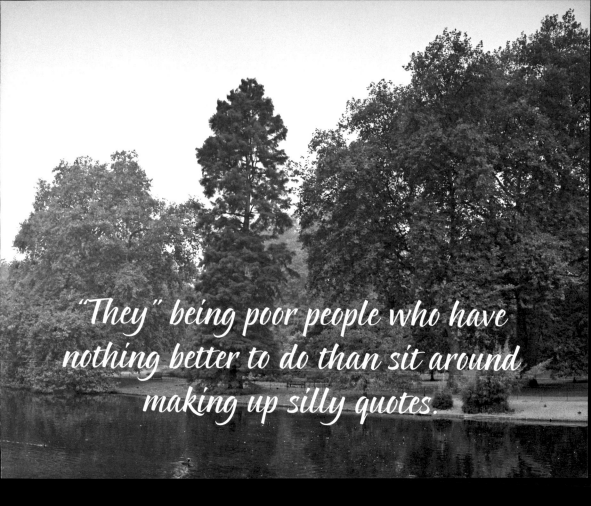

"They" being poor people who have nothing better to do than sit around making up silly quotes.

Sharing is half the fun of friendship.

Not sharing is the other half.

A friend is someone who
will help you move.

To a location that is hopefully
so far away you'll never be able to
ruin his Saturday again.

Friends don't ask friends
to dress identically for a photo.

Those are called "enemies."

I wave enthusiastically to at least one stranger I drive past a day— not to be friendly, but because I know it will confuse them.

Friends only rarely say,
"Shut up, nerd."

ROOM FOR YOUR OWN SOCIOPATHIC THOUGHTS

ROOM FOR YOUR OWN SOCIOPATHIC THOUGHTS

PHOTO CREDITS